BLESSING IN A TWEET

BLESSING IN A TWEET

RIAN MALAN

R REACH
PUBLISHERS

The Author has made every effort to trace and acknowledge sources/
resources/individuals. In the event that any images/information have
been incorrectly attributed or credited, the Author will be pleased to
rectify these omissions at the earliest opportunity.

ISBN 978-1-77636-191-5

Published by Rian Malan using Reach Publishers' services,
P O Box 1384, Wandsbeck, South Africa, 3631

Edited by Laura Grey for Reach Publishers
Cover designed by Bianca Vosloo & Reach Publishers
Website: www.reachpublishers.org
E-mail: reach@reachpublish.co.za

Rian Malan

rian@blessinginatweet.org

The characters and events portrayed in this book are
fictitious. Any similarity to real persons, living or dead, is
coincidental and not intended by the author.

He will give you the desires of your heart.

- *Psalm 37:4*

Love, trust and obey God and His Way.
Do to others as you want others to do to you.
Pray and hope through Jesus with
faith and thanksgiving.

- *Blessing In A Tweet*

Table of Contents

Introduction

"*Blessing In A Tweet* is an inspiration that emerged after reading the Holy Bible from A-Z in 2021.

Even though I grew up in a Christian house and have regarded myself as a Christian all my life, the reading had a dramatic impact on my life. It had a dramatic impact on my relationship with God.

After the reading, I asked myself, *What is your salient take on the 727,969 words you have read?*

I made a shortlist:

1. God is powerful and His wrath for disobedience is to be feared.
2. God loves those who love Him and therefore obey Him, and He blesses those who comply and punishes those who don't.
3. God loves humankind so much that He sacrificed His one and only Son, Jesus Christ, on the cross. Those who believe are saved from the wrath of

God and, therefore, from certain death.

4.   By and through this show of love, God left us with three fundamental dictates or commandments:

4.1   Love God above all else. This dictate also translates into "Obey God's commandments."

4.2   Love your neighbour as you love yourself or "Do to others as you want others to do to you."

4.3   Believe the Good News of the Gospel and engage with God through Jesus for guidance, protection and blessing.

Having written this, the next question that came up was, *What is God's 'Grand Plan' and what is my role in His plan?*

The answer I received was that the unification of Heaven and earth is the end goal of God.

The Bible divides God's plan into five phases:

Phase One: Creation of man in the image of God, ending with the fall of man in the Garden of Eden.

Phase Two: The struggle of God with an obstinate and stubborn Israel.

Phase Three: The birth, death (*"It is finished"* - John 19:30), resurrection and ascension of Jesus Christ.

Phase Four: The opportunity of humankind to buy into the Gospel of Jesus Christ.

Phase Five: The second coming of Christ when the Kingdom of God will descend to earth (*"It is done"* - Revelation 21:6).

The reading also guided me to believe that my role in God's unification plan was to work towards that unification by becoming "Godly" and proclaiming God's "Immanuel" (God saves or God rescues) deed.

How?

By living the *Blessing In A Tweet*:

Love, trust and obey God and His Way.

Do to others as you want others to do to you.

Pray and hope through Jesus with faith and thanksgiving.

Preface

"*B*lessing in A Tweet" was inspired and born during the COVID-19 years of 2020-2021. During that time, I embarked on a Bible Reading Plan on Bible Gateway and read all 727,969 words of the Bible in 90 days. When I finished, I reached out to God for help to summarize what I had read.

Verses in "*Blessing In A Tweet*" is from the New International Version (NIV) of the Holy Bible.

It is human nature to ask, *What's in it for me?* The promise of Christianity is eternal life. This promise is summed up beautifully in John 3:16, "For God so loved the world that he gave his one and only Son, that whoever believes in him shall not perish but have eternal life."

The next logical question is undoubtedly, *What does 'eternal life' mean?*

"Now this is eternal life: that they know you, the only true God, and Jesus Christ, whom you have sent." (John 17:3) Knowledge of, or rather about, God and Jesus Christ, gives eternal life. The way to get this knowledge is to go to God's Word and read it – all of it!

Currently, I enjoy a daily ritual that started on 21 June 2021 of reading the Bible (Old/New Testament) in a year, the New Testament in 24 Weeks, a Daily Verse and Proverbs Monthly. In addition, I read two Devotionals bought for me by my daughter, Michelle.

When Jesus was confronted with the question, "Teacher, what good thing must I do to get eternal life?" He answered as follows:

"Why do you ask me about what is good? There is only One who is good. If you want to enter life, keep the commandments." (Matthew 19:16-17)

God's promise, the gift or blessing of "eternal life", is therefore not unconditional. This gift from God requires us to think (mind), feel (heart) and do (action based on a decision) certain things.

From the above two verses (John 3:16, Matthew 22:36-40), essential dictates are the following:

1.   Believe in the life and death of Jesus Christ.
2.   Keep God's commandments.

The mission with *Blessing In A Tweet* was to encapsulate a Christian guideline in a Tweet of not more than 140 characters (including spaces and punctuation marks) – a Tweet that, if complied with fully, will lead to the receipt of God's blessings.

The Bible instructs us to respond to God's great love for us with our whole selves: heart, soul, mind, and strength (Mark 12:30). So, we shouldn't just focus on what we think or believe in our minds.

God's Word gives these instructions:

- "'**Love the Lord** your God with all your heart and with all your soul and with all your mind.' This is the first and greatest commandment. And the second is like it: '**Love your neighbor as yourself.**' All the Law and the Prophets hang on these two commandments." (Matthew 22:36-40)

- "In fact, this is love for God: to **keep his commands.**" (1 John 5:3)

- "May the God of hope fill you with all joy and peace as you **trust in him**, so that you may overflow with hope by the power of the Holy Spirit." (Romans 15:13)

From these verses, among other things, the first two parts of *Blessing In A Tweet* emerged:

1. **Love, trust and obey God and His Way.**

2. **Do to others as you want others to do to you.**

The following verses, among other things, led to the third part of *Blessing In A Tweet:*

- "... by **prayer** and petition, **with thanksgiving**, present your requests to God." (Philippians 4:6)

- Jesus answered, "I am the way and the truth and the life. No one comes to the Father except **through me**." (John 14:6)

- "Now **faith is confidence in what we hope for** and assurance about what we do not see." (Hebrews 11:1)

3. **Pray and hope through Jesus with faith and thanksgiving.**

As you are about to read *Blessing In A Tweet*, you may want to ask God in the name of Jesus to open your eyes, ears and heart so that you may also receive wisdom and understanding through this humble attempt to help in building God's Kingdom.

Prologue

"For I know the plans I have for you," declares
the Lord, "plans to prosper you and not to
harm you, plans to give you hope and a future."

- Jeremiah 29:11

Love, trust and obey God and His Way. Do to
others as you want others to do to you.
Pray and hope through Jesus with
faith and thanksgiving.

- Blessing In A Tweet

Promises of Blessings

The First Promise: Prosperity

Do you want this? Prosperity and hope for a better future.

Then do and live this: Love, trust and obey God and His Way. Do to others as you want others to do to you. Pray and hope through Jesus with faith and thanksgiving (*The Blessing In A Tweet*).

Key verse: "For I know the plans I have for you," declares the Lord, "plans to prosper you and not to harm you, plans to give you hope and a future" (Jeremiah 29:11).

The Bible is full of God's promises of immeasurable blessings. These promises include fulfilling all our needs and desires, prosperity, power, success, achievement, serenity (no worries), hope for a better future, strength, fearlessness, encouragement, calmness and peace.

Jeremiah 29:11 is one of God's most quoted promises. This verse was written by the prophet Jeremiah in a letter he sent from Jerusalem to the surviving elders among the exiles and the priests, the prophets and all the other people Nebuchadnezzar had carried into exile from Jerusalem to Babylon.

The promise of this verse holds true for us today: God wants us to prosper! Or, as Romans 12:2 assures us, God's will for His people is "good, pleasing and perfect."

How do we get this prosperity? Ask and it will be yours.

Key verse: "Therefore I tell you, whatever you ask for in prayer, believe that you have received it, and it will be yours" (Mark 11:24, Matthew 21:22, John 14:13-14, and Luke 11:9).

The only condition stated in Mark 11:24 is that we must have faith, namely that we must believe that we have already received what we have asked.

Jesus also assures us again in Matthew 7:7-8 that "...everyone who asks receives; the one who seeks finds; and to the one who knocks, the door will be opened."

The Second Promise:

The Desires of Your Heart

Do you want this? List the deepest desire of your heart here: _____

Then do and live this: Love, trust and obey God and His Way. Do to others as you want others to do to you. Pray and hope through Jesus with faith and thanksgiving (The Blessing In A Tweet).

Key verse: "Take delight in the Lord, and he will give you the desires of your heart" (Psalm 37:4).

God will, conditionally, give you whatever your heart desires. In Proverbs 17:3, the Bible also says that God "tests the heart." God knows the motives we have when we engage with Him. As James 4:3 puts it, "...you do not receive, because you ask with wrong motives."

The Third Promise: Anything You Ask

Do you want this? List the latest thing you asked for: _____

Then do and live this: Love, trust and obey God and His Way. Do to others as you want others to do to you. Pray and hope through Jesus with faith and thanksgiving (The Blessing In A Tweet).

Key verse: "Dear friends, if our hearts do not condemn us, we have confidence before God and receive from him anything we ask, because we keep his commands and do what pleases him" (1 John 3:21-22).

With confidence that we will get it, we can ask God for anything. There are, however, conditions: (1) Our heart must not condemn us, (2) We must keep God's commands and (3) We must do what pleases God. In John 14:14, Jesus also says, "If you ask me anything in my name, I will do it."

The Fourth Promise:
Every Need of Yours

Do you want this? List your needs: _____

    Then do and live this: Love, trust and obey God and His Way. Do to others as you want others to do to you. Pray and hope through Jesus with faith and thanksgiving (The Blessing In A Tweet).

Key verse: "And my God will supply every need of yours according to his riches in glory in Christ Jesus" (Philippians 4:19).

This promise links closely to our relationship with others and specifically also with God's law of reciprocity. In many instances, God promises to bless those who are generous and helpful towards the needy and the vulnerable. In Proverbs 11:25, this blessing is stated as follows: "A generous person will prosper; whoever refreshes others will be refreshed."

How do we receive God's promises?

Key verse: "You need to persevere so that when you have done the will of God, you will receive what he has promised" (Hebrews 10:36).

Once again, God ensures us that we will receive His many promises of eternal life, prosperity, protection against the evil one, guidance from the Holy Spirit, strength, etc. And, once again, there is the flipside of the coin, "when you have done the will of God." It is for us to fully discover what the will of God is. Then we will be able to see and experience the grace and love of God by receiving His promised blessings.

The *"Blessing In A Tweet"* will guide us on this journey of discovery and blessing.

the Tweet

Love, trust and obey God and His Way. Do to others as you want others to do to you. Pray and hope through Jesus with faith and thanksgiving.

This Tweet, exactly 140 characters, is a guideline for our lives. It comes directly from the Word of God. I was inspired over a period of six months in 2021 to put it together.

This Tweet can guide what we think, feel, and do. If we follow this tweet, it can bring great blessings.

This way of living is a law like the law of gravity – you can't ignore it or avoid it.

The Tweet contains three parts.

(I) Our lives and God
(II) Our lives and others
(III) Our lives in and through Jesus

Part I - Our lives and God

Love, trust and obey **God** and His Way. Do to others as you want others to do to you. Pray and hope through Jesus with faith and thanksgiving.

I am the Alpha and the Omega, the First and the Last, the Beginning and the End.

- Revelation 22:13

[Revelation 1:8] [Revelation 21:6]

Nobody can or will ever explain the splendour and amazement of the Creation through scientific or any other means.

On 10 May 1994, Nelson Mandela ended his inaugural presidential speech in Pretoria with: **"God bless Africa!"** He acknowledged God as the giver of blessings.

Acknowledging God, 'I AM WHO I AM' (Exodus 3:14), is a question of blind belief and faith. The moment God the Holy Spirit enters our lives, all doubt gets removed in the most dramatic of ways.

You will know it when that happens.

And it happens the moment we declare with our mouths that Jesus is Lord and believe in our hearts that God raised him from the dead. (Romans 10:9-10)

Love God

Love, trust and obey God and His Way. Do to others as you want others to do to you. Pray and hope through Jesus with faith and thanksgiving.

Love the Lord your God with all your heart and with all your soul and with all your mind and with all your strength.

- Jesus, Mark 12:30

[Deuteronomy 6:5] [1 Corinthians 8:3] [1 John 5:3] [1 John 4:19]

After having read the whole Bible in 90 days, I was left with the realisation that on the foundation of blind belief or faith are two pillars. The first is the promise of unimaginable blessing. The second is the prerequisite of unquestionable obedience to God's commandments.

God the Son (Jesus) said about loving God, "This is the first and greatest commandment." But how do you love

God? The answer was given to us in 1 John 5:3, "In fact, this is love for God: to keep His commands."

Trust God

Love, trust and obey God and His Way. Do to others as you want others to do to you. Pray and hope through Jesus with faith and thanksgiving.

...and blessed is the one who trusts in the Lord.

- Proverbs 16:20

[Romans 15:13]

The Tweet is about asking God for blessing, and a prerequisite is that we have to trust that God can provide what we ask. Trust means that there must never be a shadow of a doubt that God can deliver the blessing.

God will fill us with confident expectations compared to wishful thinking. We just have to trust Him fully.

33

Obey God and His Way

Love, trust and **obey God and His Way**.
Do to others as you want others to do
to you. Pray and hope through Jesus with
faith and thanksgiving.

Blessed rather are those who hear the word of God and obey it.

- Luke 11:28

[1 John 5:3] [Psalm 128:1] [Proverbs 8:32] [Romans 11:22] [Micah 6:8]

The Bible is full of narratives of the consequences of disobedience to the Word of God. When we obey God, there are showers of blessings. When we disobey, there are consequences and punishment.

The first and greatest commandment is that we must love God, and it has been clearly shown to us that love for God is nothing else but to obey God.

Love and obey God

Love, trust and obey God and His Way. Do to others as you want others to do to you. Pray and hope through Jesus with faith and thanksgiving.

In fact, this is love for God: to keep his commands.

- 1 John 5:3

[Deuteronomy 10:12]

When Jesus was asked what the greatest commandment was, he replied:

"'Love the Lord your God with all your heart and with all your soul and with all your mind.' This is the first and greatest commandment." (Matthew 22:36-40).

With that He said:

[Love for God] = [Keep God's commandment]

Part II - Our Lives and Others

Love, trust and obey God and His Way. **Do to others as you want others to do to you.** Pray and hope through Jesus with faith and thanksgiving.

So in everything, do to others what you would have them do to you, for this sums up the Law and the Prophets.

- Jesus, Matthew 7:12

[Leviticus 19:18] [Matthew 19:19] [Matthew 22:39] [Mark 12:31] [Mark 12:33] [Luke 10:27] [Romans 13:9] [Galatians 5:14] [James 2:8]

Some describe this commandment as the "Golden Rule". It is also stated as follows, "Love your neighbour as yourself." (Matthew 19:19). In James 2:8, it is called "the royal law".

It is, in fact, the most practical guideline, or rather commandment. We must make it second nature.

We just have to ask ourselves:

Would we have liked someone else to do to us what we are about to do to them?

Part III - Our Lives
in and through Jesus

Love, trust and obey God and His Way. Do to others as you want others to do to you. Pray and hope through Jesus with faith and thanksgiving.

For God so loved the world that he gave his one and only Son (Jesus), that whoever believes in him shall not perish but have eternal life.

- John 3:16

[Isaiah 9:6-7] [John 14:6] [1 Timothy 2:5] [Ephesians 2:8-9]

Jesus is the Son of God.

He is also part of the triune God – the Father, Son and Holy Ghost. He was present when God created everything. Jesus is also the gift from God who was sent as a human being to die on the cross for our sins so we may have eternal life with the only condition being that we believe in Him.

In the Apostles' Creed, the statement of faith about Jesus is as follows:

I believe in Jesus Christ, his only Son, our Lord,
    who was conceived by the Holy Spirit
    and born of the virgin Mary.
    He suffered under Pontius Pilate,
    was crucified, died, and was buried;
    he descended to hell.
    The third day he rose again from the dead.
    He ascended to heaven
    and is seated at the right hand of God the Father almighty.
    From there he will come to judge the living and the dead.

The Bible Gateway makes this Statement of Faith about Jesus:

Doctrine of Christ. Jesus Christ, the second Person of the Trinity, was conceived by the Holy Spirit, born of the Virgin Mary — he was God in human flesh. He lived a sinless human life, yet willingly took upon himself our sins by dying in our place and on our behalf. He rose bodily, victorious over death. He ascended to Heaven and is at the right hand of the Father as the believer's advocate and mediator. Some day, he will return to consummate history and to fulfil the eternal plan of God.

Pray

Love, trust and obey God and His Way. Do to others as you want others to do to you. Pray and hope through Jesus with faith and thanksgiving.

And pray in the Spirit on all occasions with all kinds of prayers and requests.

- Ephesians 6:18

If God knows what we need before we ask Him, why pray? Because He instructs us to come to Him in prayer and as such acknowledge our dependence on the Him and to give Him His glory.

God chose to use prayer as a way to fulfil His purpose. It is important to pray with adoration, confession, thanksgiving and supplication.

Jesus (Matthew 6:7-13) gave us the following guideline for praying:

"And when you pray, do not be like the hypocrites, for they love to pray standing in the synagogues and on the street corners to be seen by others. Truly I tell you, they have received their reward in full. But when you pray, go into your room, close the door and pray to your Father, who is unseen. Then your Father, who sees what is done in secret, will reward you. And when you pray, do not keep on babbling like pagans, for they think they will be heard because of their many words. Do not be like them, for your Father knows what you need before you ask him."

This, then, is how you should pray:

Our Father in heaven,
hallowed be your name,
your kingdom come,
your will be done,
on earth as it is in heaven.

Give us today our daily bread.

And forgive us our debts,
as we also have forgiven our debtors.

And lead us not into temptation,
but deliver us from the evil one.

For yours is the kingdom and the power and the glory forever.

Rejoice always, pray continually, give thanks in all circumstances; for this is God's will for you in Christ Jesus. (1 Thessalonians 5:16-18)

through Jesus. . .

Love, trust and obey God and His Way.
Do to others as you want others to do
to you. Pray and hope **through Jesus**
with faith and thanksgiving.

... always giving thanks to God the
Father for everything, in the name of
our Lord Jesus Christ.

- Ephesians 5:20

[John 14:6] [John 16:23] [1 Timothy 2:5] [Ephesians 2:8-9]

Jesus gave us the guideline when he said, "Very truly I
tell you, my Father will give you whatever you ask in my
name." (John 16:23).

He also made it very clear that He is "... the way and the
truth and the life. No one comes to the Father except
through me." (John 14:6)

Pray with thanksgiving. . .

Love, trust and obey God and His Way. Do to others as you want others to do to you. Pray and hope through Jesus with faith and thanksgiving.

Do not be anxious about anything, but in every situation, by prayer and petition, with thanksgiving, present your requests to God.

- Philippians 4:6

[1 Thessalonians 5:16-18] [Hebrews 13:15] [Psalm 100:4] [Ephesians 5:20]

Praying with thanksgiving is not only a commandment, but it is also an acknowledgement of the essential elements of hope, trust and faith that God will answer our prayers.

When we pray, we must thank God for His love, grace, guidance, protection AND for hearing our prayer and petition.

Pray with Faith

Love, trust and obey God and His Way. Do to others as you want others to do to you. Pray and hope through Jesus with faith and thanksgiving.

Therefore I tell you, whatever you ask for in prayer, believe that you have received it, and it will be yours.

- Mark 11:24

[Hebrews 11:1] [Romans 12:12]

The Bible aptly describes faith as "confidence in what we hope for and assurance about what we do not see." (Hebrews 11:1]).

Indeed, if Jesus says that God will give us whatever we ask in Jesus' name and if we don't believe what He says, it is a flagrant rejection of God's Word.

Hope

Love, trust and obey God and His Way. Do to others as you want others to do to you. Pray and hope through Jesus with faith and thanksgiving.

… but those who hope in the Lord will renew their strength. They will soar on wings like eagles…

- Isaiah 40:31

[Psalm 147:11] [Proverbs 23:18]

"Hope" suggests confidence or assurance in the possibility that what one desires or longs for will happen.

In Psalms, the Bible states that "The Lord delights in those who fear him, who put their hope in his unfailing love." (Psalm 147:11)

Blessing In A Tweet - Quo Vadis?

"For I know the plans I have for you," declares the Lord, "plans to prosper you and not to harm you, plans to give you hope and a future."

- Jeremiah 29:11

Love, trust and obey God and His Way. Do to others as you want others to do to you. Pray and hope through Jesus with faith and thanksgiving.

- Blessing In A Tweet

God wants to bless us in ways that we can hardly imagine - here and now.

The great blessing of eternal life (John 17:3) is not a promise of life after death – it was given to us by the grace of God after the death and resurrection of Jesus Christ.

When we declare with our mouths that Jesus is Lord and believe in our hearts that God raised him from the dead, we are saved (Romans 10:9-10) and we then open ourselves to receive the promises and blessings from God. .

God wants us to prosper, and He wants to bless us (Isaiah 30:18).

But there are conditions to receiving God's grace and blessings.

We have to:

- Love God above all and love others as we love ourselves.
- Obey God's commandments.
- Trust in God. That is, we must have a steadfast belief that we can ask and receive anything from God.
- Believe in the Gospel of Jesus Christ and approach God in prayer through Jesus. and
- Accompany our requests to God with thanksgiving as though we have already received it, that is, with absolute faith.

Love, trust and obey God and His Way. Do to others as you want others to do to you. Pray and hope through Jesus with faith and thanksgiving.

Blessing

May the Lord:

Bless you
   and keep you.
Make his face shine on you
   and be gracious to you.
Turn his face toward you
   and give you peace.

- (Numbers 6:24-26)

Epilogue

Lord, give us the wisdom and understanding of how you want us to love, trust and obey You and Your Way.

Guide us in our daily connections with others to indeed do to them as we want them to do to us.

God Almighty, empower us to have unwavering hope and faith that you will bless us abundantly.

We thank you, Lord, that You have heard our prayer and that You will fulfil it according to Your will.

We ask this all in Jesus' name.

Amen

Acknowledgements

M y thanksgiving first and foremost goes to God for showering me with guidance from the Holy Spirit, for giving me the strength to soar like an eagle, for giving me the patience to persevere.

Soli Deo Gloria

One of the biggest blessings I ever received was my beloved wife. Thank you, Beatrice, for enduring my sometimes annoying testing of thoughts with you and not insisting that I must do chores while engulfed in *Blessing In A Tweet*.

Without the blessed tool of Bible Gateway Online, the compilation of this humble contribution to God's work would have been cumbersome.

Rudolf Markgraaf of TheXchange/Turncoin/VirtualStaX, thank you for listening to God's call to invite me for that divine moment at Wedderville in March of 2021 – a moment that sparked the journey towards *Blessing In A Tweet*.

The blessed assessment you did for me, Alyson Rockhold, gave me some comfort that at least one person other than myself has found the *Blessing In A Tweet* of value.

Statements of Faith

*B*lessing *In A Tweet* is an inspired guideline for living a life that will lead to the receipt of God's blessings with the promise of eternal life as core to Christianity.

The following statements of faith are added to this writing as acknowledgement that *Blessing In A Tweet* must be read in the context of the Word of God – the whole Word.

Statement Of Faith For Bible Gateway

Doctrine of Scripture. The Bible is God's unique revelation to mankind, the inspired, infallible Word of God. As such, it is the supreme and final authority and without error in what it teaches and affirms. No other writings are vested with such divine authority.

Doctrine of God. There is only one true God. He exists eternally as three persons — Father, Son and Holy Spirit — each fully God yet each personally distinct from the other. God is the creator of everything.

Doctrine of Sin. Everyone, regardless of race, gender, social class or intellectual ability, is created in God's image and for communion with God. But because of sin, that communion was broken and all of humanity was separated from God, the source of all life. Because of the fall, everyone deserves God's judgement.

Doctrine of Salvation. Jesus Christ is the Way, the Truth, and the Life, and God gives salvation and eternal life to those who trust in Him. Salvation cannot be earned through personal goodness or human effort. It is a gift that is received by repentance and faith in Christ and His death on the cross and resurrection from the grave.

Doctrine of Christ. Jesus Christ, the second Person of the Trinity, was conceived by the Holy Spirit, born of the Virgin Mary — he was God in human flesh. He lived a sinless human life, yet willingly took upon Himself our sins by dying in our place and on our behalf. He rose bodily, victorious over death. He ascended to Heaven and is at the right hand of the Father as the believer's advocate and mediator. One day, He will return to consummate history and to fulfil the eternal plan of God.

Doctrine of the Holy Spirit. The Holy Spirit, the third Person of the Trinity, convicts the world of sin and gives new life to those who trust in Jesus. He indwells all believers and is available to empower them to lead Christ-like lives. The Spirit gives them spiritual gifts with which to serve fellow believers and reach out to a lost and needy world.

Doctrine of Judgement. At the final judgement, unbelievers will be separated from God into condemnation. Believers will be received into God's loving presence.

Doctrine of the Church. All believers are members of the body of Christ, the one true church universal. Spiritual unity is to be expressed among Christians by acceptance and love of one another across ethnic, cultural, socio-economic, national, generational, gender and denominational lines. The local church is a group of believers who gather for worship, prayer, instruction, encouragement, mutual accountability, community with each other and as a witness to the world.

Apostles' Creed

I believe in God, the Father almighty,
    creator of heaven and earth.

I believe in Jesus Christ, his only Son, our Lord,
    who was conceived by the Holy Spirit
    and born of the virgin Mary.
    He suffered under Pontius Pilate,
    was crucified, died, and was buried;
    he descended to hell.
    The third day he rose again from the dead.
    He ascended to heaven
    and is seated at the right hand of God the Father
    almighty.
    From there he will come to judge the living and the
    dead.

I believe in the Holy Spirit,
    the holy catholic* church,
    the communion of saints,
    the forgiveness of sins,
    the resurrection of the body,
    and the life everlasting. Amen.

*that is, the true Christian church of all times and all places